ESSENTIAL ELEMENTS®

GUITAR ENSEMBLES

ROCK HITS

CONTENTS

Arrangements by Chip Henderson and Mark Phillips

ISBN 978-1-4584-1590-5

Visit Hal Leonard Online at
www.halleonard.com

Contact us:
Hal Leonard
7777 West Bluemound Road
Milwaukee, WI 53213
Email: info@halleonard.com

In Europe, contact:
Hal Leonard Europe Limited
42 Wigmore Street
Marylebone, London, W1U 2RN
Email: info@halleonardeurope.com

In Australia, contact:
Hal Leonard Australia Pty. Ltd.
4 Lentara Court
Cheltenham, Victoria, 3192 Australia
Email: info@halleonard.com.au

ALL THE SMALL THINGS

Words and Music by Tom De Longe and Mark Hoppus

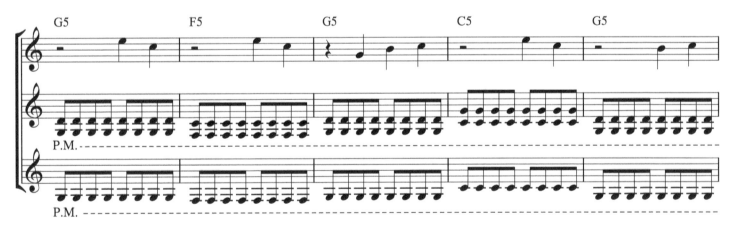

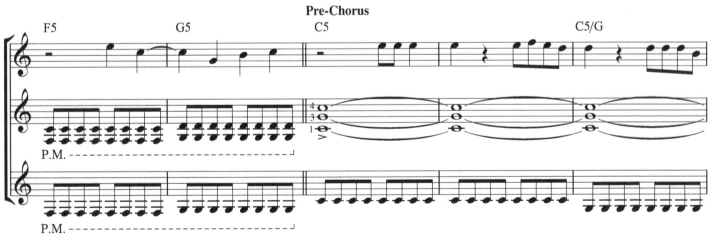

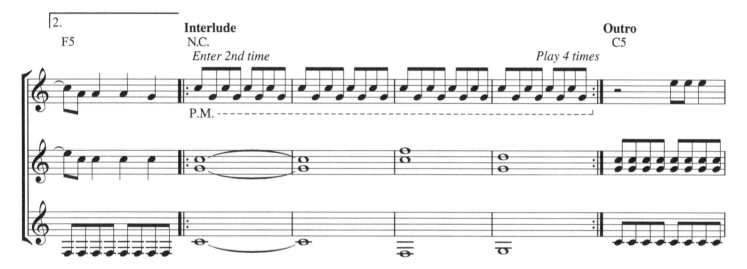

BEAUTIFUL DAY

Words by Bono
Music by U2

Bridge 1

Bridge 2

Outro

BEST OF YOU

Words and Music by Dave Grohl, Taylor Hawkins, Chris Shiflett and Nate Mendel

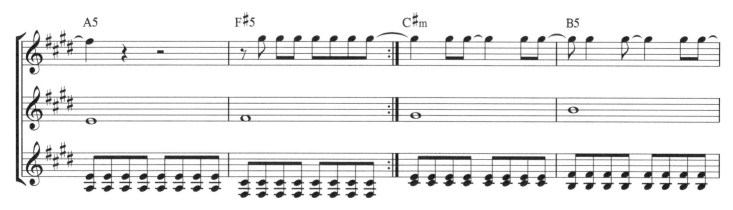

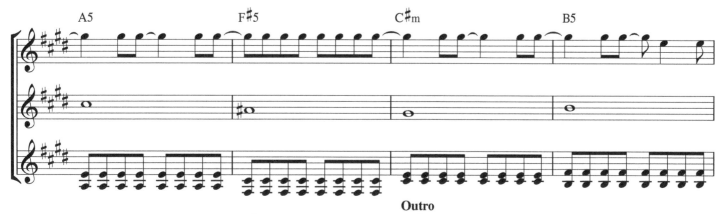

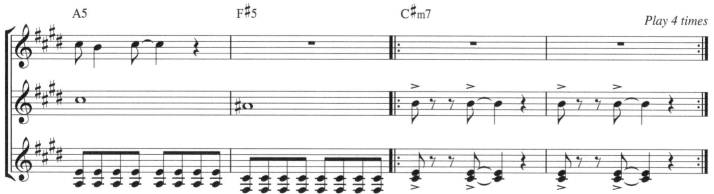

CLOCKS

Words and Music by Guy Berryman, Jon Buckland, Will Champion and Chris Martin

Intro
Moderately fast

Verse

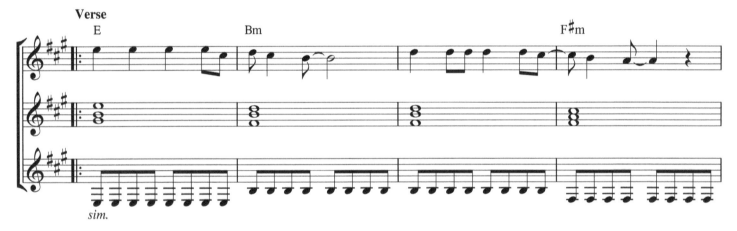

Chorus

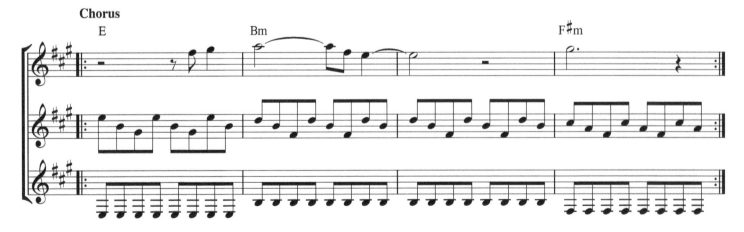

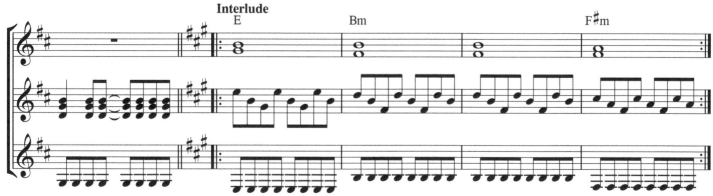

HEY, SOUL SISTER

Words and Music by Pat Monahan, Espen Lind and Amund Bjorkland

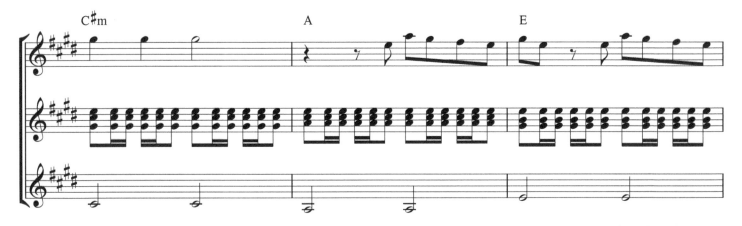

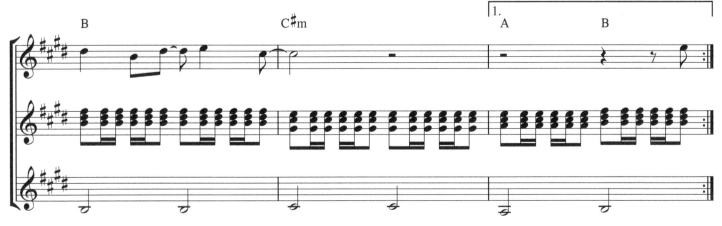

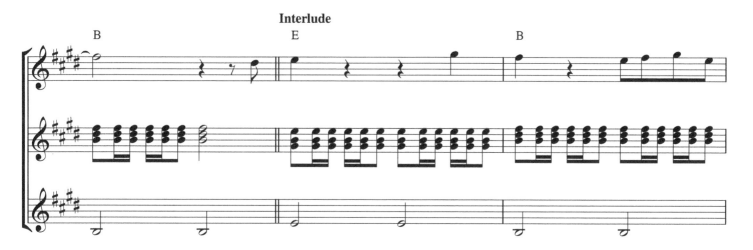

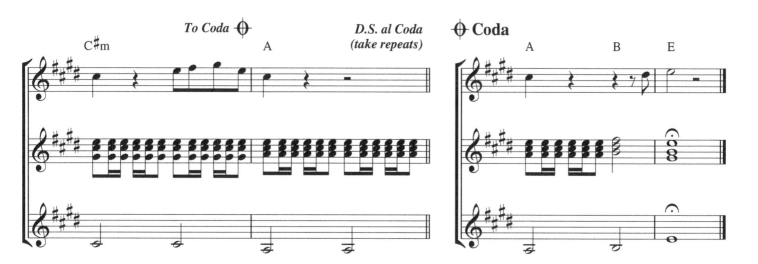

IRIS

from the Motion Picture CITY OF ANGELS

Words and Music by John Rzeznik

Intro

Moderately fast

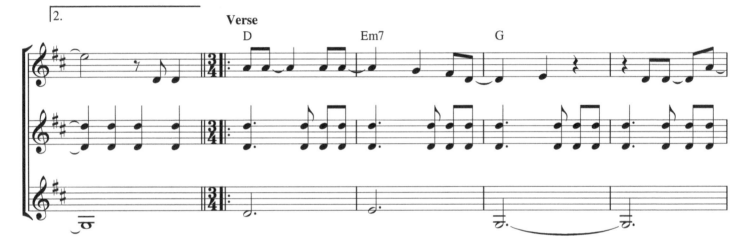

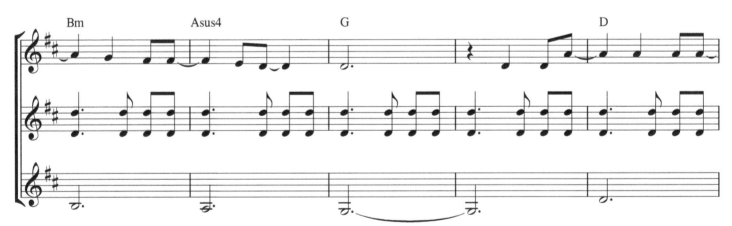

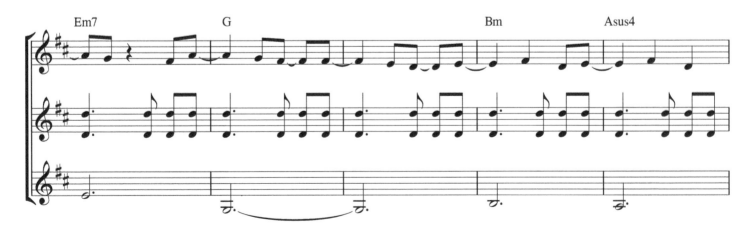

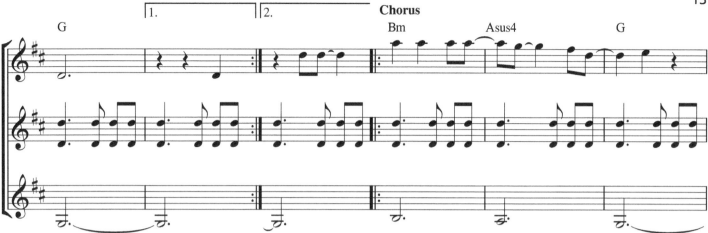

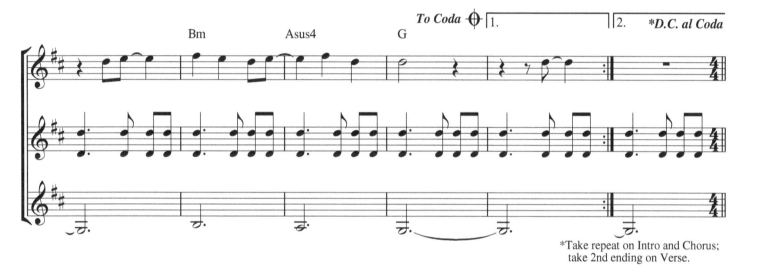

*Take repeat on Intro and Chorus;
take 2nd ending on Verse.

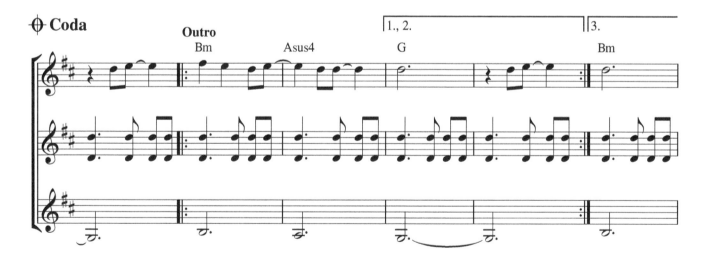

PLUSH

Words and Music by Scott Weiland, Dean DeLeo, Robert DeLeo and Eric Kretz

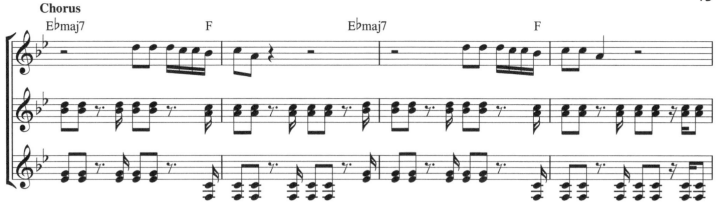

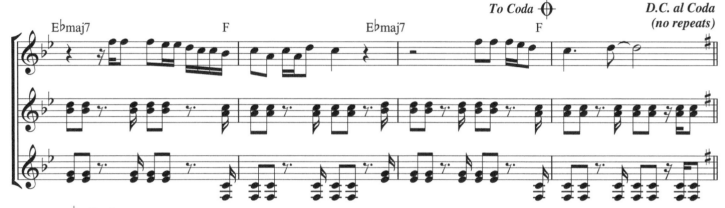

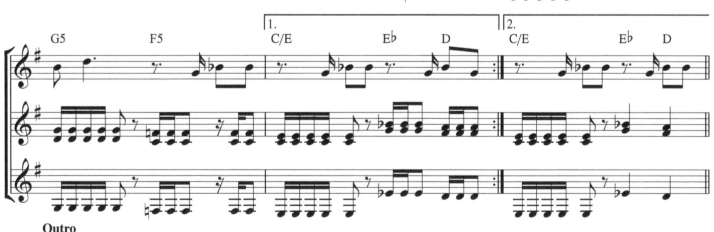

SAY IT AIN'T SO

Words and Music by Rivers Cuomo

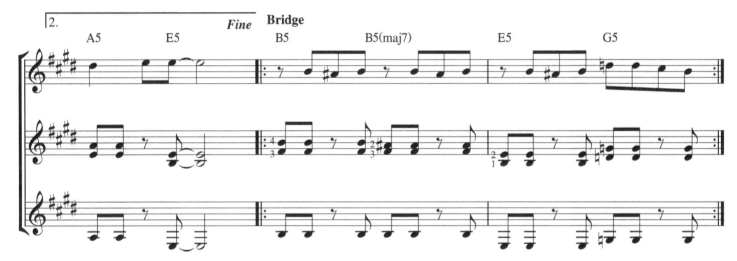

SMELLS LIKE TEEN SPIRIT

Words and Music by Kurt Cobain, Krist Novoselic and Dave Grohl

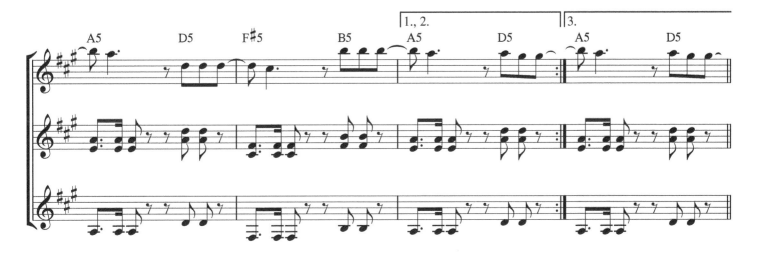

SMOOTH

Words by Rob Thomas
Music by Rob Thomas and Itaal Shur

Pre-Chorus

Chorus

To Coda ⊕   *D.C. al Coda*
                    (take repeat)

⊕ **Coda**   **Outro**

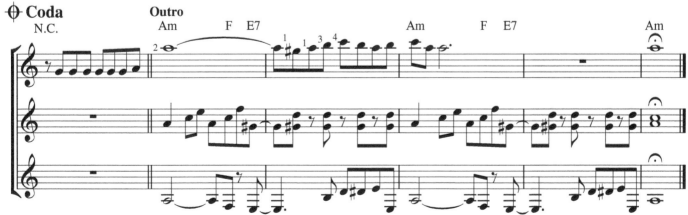

THIS LOVE

Words and Music by Adam Levine and Jesse Carmichael

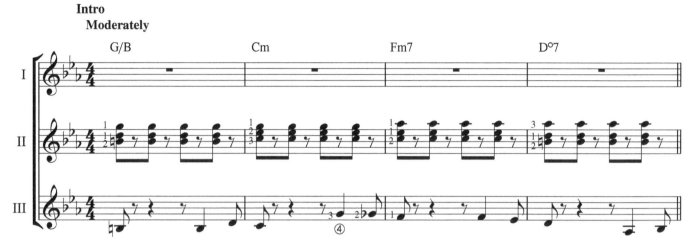

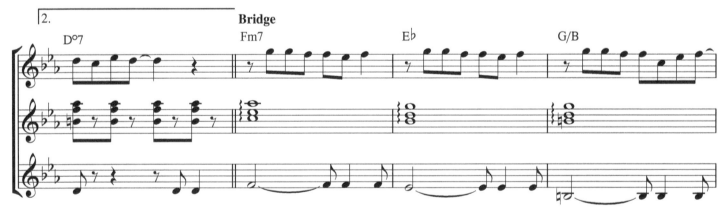

21 GUNS

Words and Music by David Bowie, John Phillips, Billie Joe and Green Day

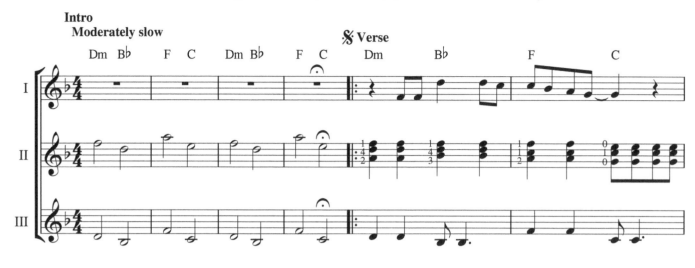

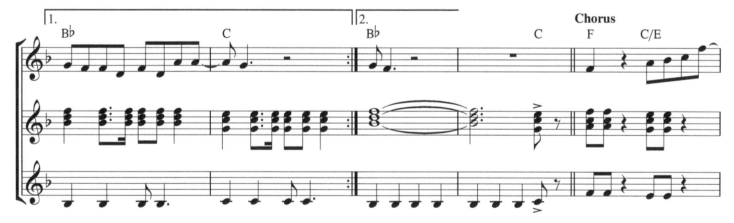

To Coda

1st time, D.S. al Coda
(take repeat)
2nd time, Fine

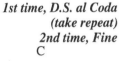

Coda

Bridge

Interlude

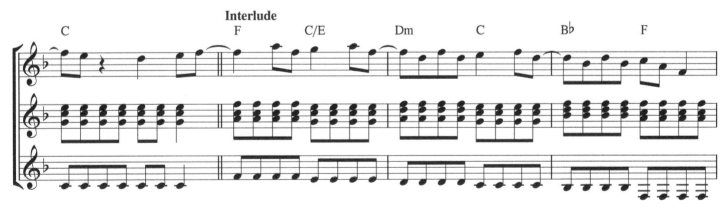

D.S. al Fine
(take 2nd ending)

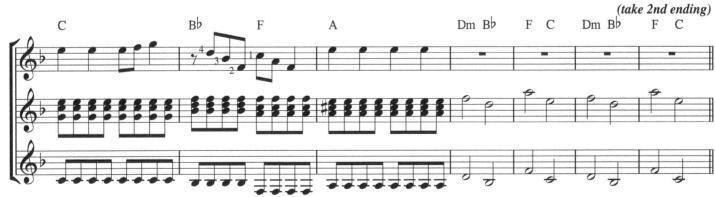

USE SOMEBODY

Words and Music by Caleb Followill, Nathan Followill, Jared Followill and Matthew Followill

Intro/Chorus
Moderately fast

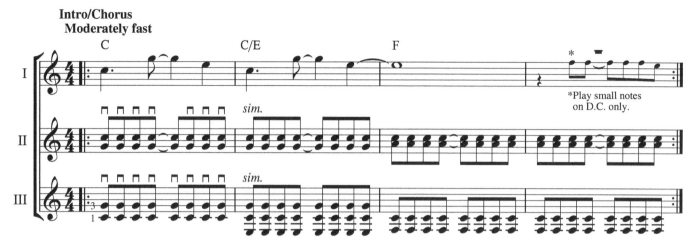

*Play small notes on D.C. only.

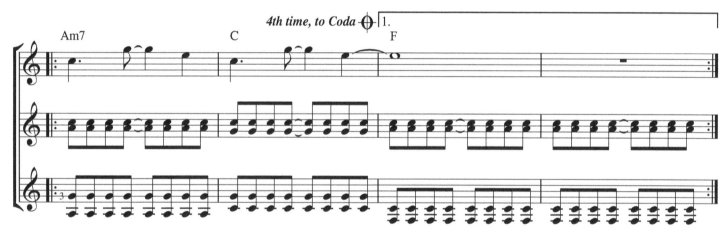

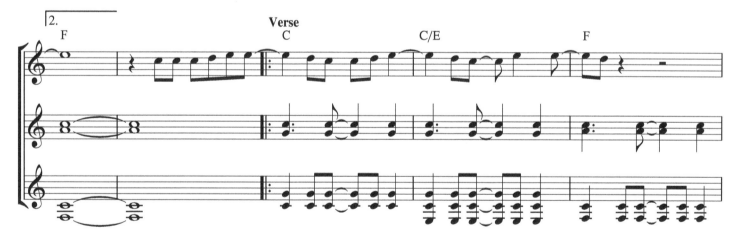

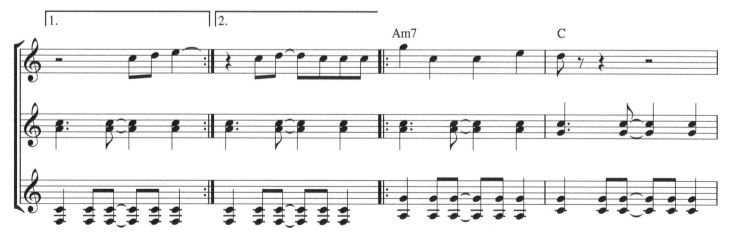

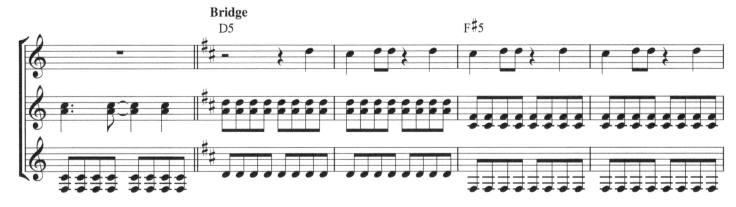

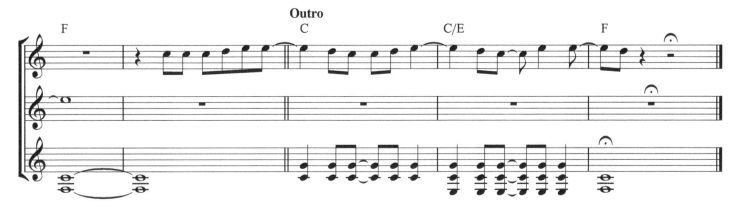

WONDERWALL

Words and Music by Noel Gallagher

Intro
Moderately fast

% Verse

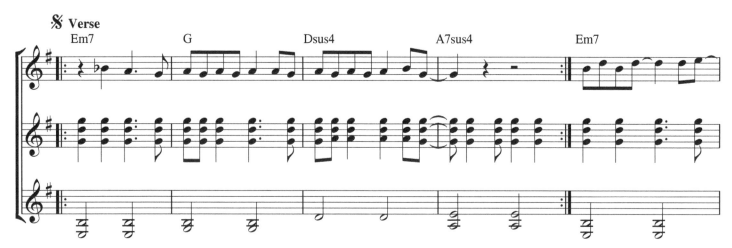

Pre-Chorus

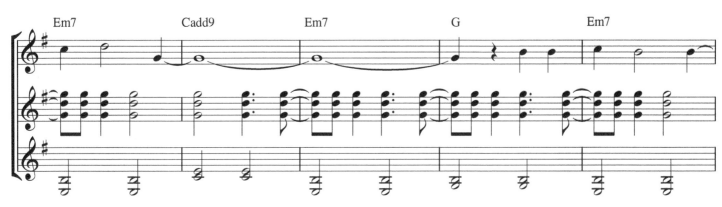

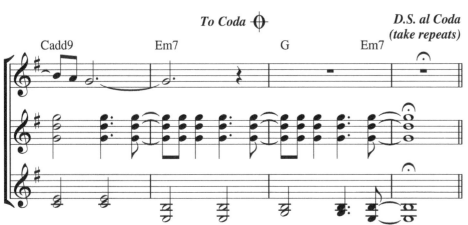

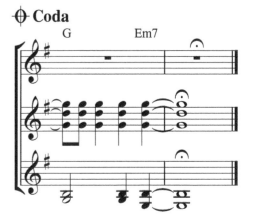

UNDER THE BRIDGE

Words and Music by Anthony Kiedis, Flea, John Frusciante and Chad Smith

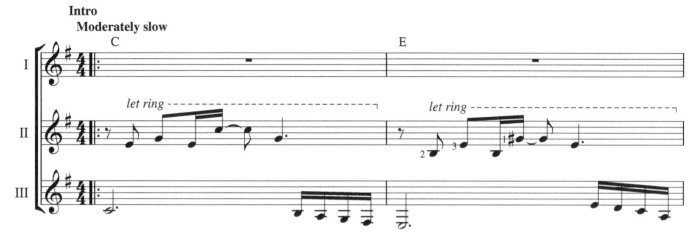